Contents

Fiction
Kidnapped!
page 2

Play
Rats in the Cellar
page 22

Poem
My Baby Brother
page 28

Non-fiction
Deadly Diseases
page 30

Written by
Alison Hawes

Illustrated by
Amerigo Pinelli

Series editor **Dee Reid**

Before reading
Kidnapped!

Characters

Lily

Ralf

A stranger

A woman

Tricky words

ch1 p3	whistled	
ch1 p4	townspeople	
ch2 p7	politely	
ch2 p10	queue	
ch2 p11	wriggling	
ch3 p13	search	
ch3 p14	cellar	
ch4 p19	plague	

Story starter

The plague had killed Lily's parents and now she had to look after her baby brother, Ralf. Lily's father had been a rat catcher and Lily was on her way to town to get work as a rat catcher. A stranger driving a cart offered Lily a lift but Snapper, Lily's dog, barked at the man and Lily chose to walk instead.

Kidnapped!

Chapter One

Every day, Lily put her father's rat traps on her back. Then she picked up her baby brother, Ralf, whistled for her dog, Snapper, and went to find work.

Most people Lily worked for paid her with food, but her rent was due and she needed money to pay it. So Lily walked into town. It was a long way from home, but the townspeople had given her father a penny for every ten rats he caught. Lily hoped they would do the same for her.

It was hot and
as soon as they walked
out of the woods, Ralf
started crying.
Lily kept stopping so they could
all drink the water she had brought,
but soon the stone bottle was empty
and there was still a long way to go.

Then a cart bumped along the road. It slowed down as it came closer. Lily looked up, hoping it was a friend from the village on their way into town, but the man on the cart was a stranger.

Chapter Two

"Morning, Miss," said the man. "That's a bonny baby you have there. Would you like a lift into town?"

Snapper growled at the man.

"No, thank you," Lily replied politely. "We're happy to walk."

"As you wish," said the man, and he went on his way.

As soon as they reached town, Lily went to the well in the square to get a drink for them all. It was hot and crowded by the well, so Lily put Ralf in a shady spot under a tree.

"Stay!" Lily ordered Snapper, pointing at Ralf in his basket. Snapper lay down next to Ralf and didn't move. Once Lily was sure that Ralf was safe, she went over to the well and waited for her turn to fill her bottle.

When she got to the front of the queue, Lily heard Snapper barking loudly. Then suddenly the barking stopped. Lily rushed back to the tree but Ralf and Snapper had vanished.

Lily looked all around. She saw the cart that had passed her earlier. In the back of the cart she could just make out Ralf's basket, and next to it was a sack that was wriggling wildly.

Chapter Three

Lily screamed. She ran after the cart, but it disappeared into the crowded streets.

"Have you seen a cart with a baby?" she asked everyone she passed.

No one had.

Lily sat down outside an inn and began to cry.

"Are you alright, Miss?" said a voice behind her.
Lily stood up and wiped away her tears.
"No, sir," said Lily. "I need work and a place to stay while I search for my missing baby brother."
"Alright," said the innkeeper, "you can work for me."

Lily caught rats in the innkeeper's cellar but she spent every spare moment looking for Ralf and Snapper.

On the third day, Lily was searching on the edge of town when she saw a dog lying next to a high garden wall. It was Snapper. He was weak and hungry and his coat was matted with mud.

Lily bent down and hugged him gently. Snapper wagged his tail. He seemed so pleased to see her.

Then Lily heard a baby crying on the other side of the wall.

"I knew you wouldn't leave Ralf!" she said to Snapper.

Chapter Four

Lily opened the gate and went into the garden. She saw a woman holding a crying baby. The woman turned and looked at Lily.

"What do you think you're doing?" she shouted. "Get out of my garden!"

"Not until you give me back my brother!" said Lily.

"What do you mean, your brother?" the woman cried, holding the baby tightly to her. "This is my son!"

As soon as the baby heard Lily's voice, he stopped crying and held out his arms to her.

Then Lily hugged Ralf, whistled for Snapper and they all set off for the town.

Quiz

Text detective

- **p7** Why did Lily not tell the stranger the truth about wanting a lift to town?
- **p8** Why did Lily leave Ralf and Snapper under a tree?
- **p11** Why was the sack 'wriggling wildly'?
- **p13** Find evidence that the innkeeper is kind.
- **p17–19** Why did the woman lie about Ralf being her son?

Word detective

- **p7** Which adverb tells you that Lily is slightly nervous as she speaks to the stranger?
- **p10** Find a word that means 'disappeared'.
- **p14** Which adjectives reveal what has happened to Snapper since he was put in the sack?

What do you think?

Should Lily have left Ralf with only Snapper to take care of him? Is she a good and caring older sister? What is the evidence for your opinions?

HA! HA!

Q: What do footballers and babies have in common?

A: They both dribble!

Before reading
Rats in the Cellar

Characters

- Innkeeper
- Gavin – a boy who works at the inn
- Lily – a rat catcher

Setting the scene

Lily's baby brother, Ralf, has been kidnapped. Lily needs some work as a rat catcher so she can pay for food and a bed at night while she searches for Ralf. The innkeeper is kind to Lily but Gavin is rather grumpy.

Rats in the Cellar

Innkeeper: See what that young lady wants.

Gavin: I'm busy.

Innkeeper: Go now, Gavin, and *please* be polite to her.

Gavin: I'm always polite.
(goes outside) Can I help you, Miss?

Lily: Have you seen a man with a baby?

Gavin: I'm too busy to notice everyone who goes past!

Lily: *(in tears)* It's just that my …

Innkeeper: *(rushing outside)* Gavin, I didn't ask you to make her cry!

Lily: I just asked if …

Innkeeper:	Be quiet, Gavin.
Gavin:	But it's true! A rat ran past me when I went to get the food.
Innkeeper:	Get back to work, Gavin – now!
Lily:	Please take the money for my food and bed out of my pay.
Innkeeper:	Don't worry about that now. Just eat up. Then you can catch the rats in the kitchen. You can leave the rats in the cellar until tomorrow.

Lily: Yes, sir.

Gavin: Hey! That's not fair! I sleep in that cellar.

Innkeeper: Yes it is fair. You made the young lady cry! Now, get back to work!

Quiz

Play detective

p23 Why do you think the word 'please' is in italics?

p23 What evidence is there that Gavin is rather grumpy?

p23 How do you think Lily would finish the sentence 'It's just that my …'?

p26 What evidence is there that the innkeeper is kind?

p27 Why is Gavin even grumpier at the end of the play?

Before reading
My Baby Brother

Setting the scene

There are some adorable things about babies – their soft skin and silky hair – but not everything about babies is sweet! There are two verses in the poem separated by a short lullaby.

Poem top tip

Emphasise the rhyming words to keep the rhythm. Read the lullaby lines in a whisper as if helping the baby to sleep. Pause before reading the last line of the poem to bring out the humour.

Quiz

Poem detective

- Do you think the poem gives us a real picture of what babies are like?
- What does the poet mean when she says the baby is 'milky'?
- Why has the poet used lots of words that have the sound 's'?
- Which word rhymes with 'kick'?

My Baby Brother

My baby brother is warm and milky.
His skin is soft. His hair is silky.
He waves his tiny arms and feet.
My baby brother is soft and sweet.

Sleepy baby. Sleepy brother.
Sweet dreams, sleepy baby brother.

My baby brother is warm and milky.
His skin is soft. His hair is silky.
He waves his arms. His feet just kick.
He burps his milk and he is sick.

by Celia Warren

The Plague

The plague is a deadly disease. Millions of people died from it in medieval times.

What happens?

First, you get swollen glands. Then you suffer severe pain. You get a fever and you vomit blood. After a few days, you die.

The plague is sometimes called the Black Death.

How do you get the plague?

The plague is spread by fleas that are infected with plague bacteria. The fleas sometimes live on rats.

Is there a cure?

There was no cure for the plague in medieval times but it can usually be cured now.

Cholera

Cholera is a deadly disease. Millions of people all over the world have died from it. You catch it by drinking water infected with deadly bacteria.

In Britain in Victorian times, lots of people died from cholera. This was because many people drank water from the same river that took away their sewage.

What happens?
First you suffer from severe stomach pain. Then you get diarrhoea and vomiting.

Do people get better?
There are now vaccines against cholera, but in some countries they cost a lot of money.

Vaccines

You have probably had some vaccines. Usually a doctor or nurse gives you an injection. Some people do not like injections, but they are better than getting a deadly disease!

Not all vaccines are given by injection. You swallow the vaccine against polio.

Quiz

Text detective

p31 Why are some diseases no longer so deadly?

p35 Why did so many people die from cholera in Victorian times?

p35 Why might some people still die from cholera in some countries?

p37 Why do people still get flu even if they have had a flu vaccine?

Non-fiction features

p32 Which time connectives show the order in which things happen if you catch the plague?

p35 How has the author used the sub-headings to draw the reader into the text?

What do you think?

Apart from the use of vaccines, why might some diseases no longer kill so many people? What can people do to protect themselves from serious diseases?

HA! HA!

Q: What can you catch but not throw?

A: A cold!

Published by Pearson Education Limited, a company incorporated in England and Wales, having its registered office at Edinburgh Gate, Harlow, Essex, CM20 2JE.
Registered company number: 872828

www.pearsonschools.co.uk

Pearson is a registered trademark of Pearson plc

Text © Pearson Education Limited 2013

The right of Alison Hawes to be identified as the author of this work has been asserted by her in accordance with the Copyright, Designs and Patents Act 1988.

First published 2013

2022
13

British Library Cataloguing in Publication Data is available from the British Library on request.

ISBN: 978 0 435 15231 4

Copyright notice
All rights reserved. No part of this publication may be reproduced in any form or by any means (including photocopying or storing it in any medium by electronic means and whether or not transiently or incidentally to some other use of this publication) without the written permission of the copyright owner, except in accordance with the provisions of the Copyright, Designs and Patents Act 1988 or under the terms of a licence issued by the Copyright Licensing agency, Saffron House, 6-10 Kirby Street, London ECIN 8TS (www.cla.co.uk). Applications for the copyright owner's written permission should be addressed to the publisher.

Designed by Bigtop
Original illustrations © Pearson Education Limited 2013
Illustrated by Amerigo Pinelli
Printed and bound in the UK
Font © Pearson Education Ltd
Teaching notes by Dee Reid
Picture research by Suzannah Morris

Acknowledgements
We would like to thank the following schools for their invaluable help in the development and trialling of this course:
Callicroft Primary School, Bristol; Castlehill Primary School, Fife; Elmlea Junior School, Bristol; Lancaster School, Essex; Llanidloes School, Powys; Moulton School, Newmarket; Platt C of E Primary School, Kent; Sherborne Abbey CE VC Primary School, Dorset; Upton Junior School, Poole; Whitmore Park School, Coventry.

The author and publisher would like to thank the following individuals and organisations for permission to reproduce photographs:

(Key: b-bottom; c-centre; l-left; r-right; t-top)

Alamy Images: BSIP SA 31; **Bridgeman Art Library Ltd:** Look and Learn 32;
Getty Images: Nick Hawkins 34; **Science Photo Library Ltd:** National Museum of Health and Medicine 36; **Shutterstock.com:** Cosmin Manci 33; **Veer/Corbis:** Brad Wynnyk 37, Phuchong Choksamai 38
All other images © Pearson Education

Every effort has been made to contact copyright holders of material reproduced in this book. Any omissions will be rectified in subsequent printings if notice is given to the publishers.